WHEN THE HEART NEEDS A STUNT DOUBLE

Made in Michigan Writers Series

GENERAL EDITORS

Michael Delp, Interlochen Center for the Arts
M. L. Liebler, Wayne State University

A complete listing of the books in this series can be found online at wsupress.wayne.edu.

WHEN THE HEART NEEDS A STUNT DOUBLE

POEMS BY DIANE DECILLIS

WAYNE STATE UNIVERSITY PRESS
DETROIT

ISBN 978-0-8143-4832-1 (paperback)
ISBN 978-0-8143-4833-8 (e-book)

Library of Congress Control Number: 2020946415

Publication of this book was made possible by a generous gift from The Meijer Foundation.

On cover: *Explicit Introspection* by Rafal Olbinski. Used by permission of the artist.
Cover design by Genna Blackburn

Wayne State University Press
Leonard N. Simons Building
4809 Woodward Avenue
Detroit, Michigan 48201-1309

Visit us online at wsupress.wayne.edu

For the hearts of my heart.
You know who you are.

CONTENTS

II

III

Something About Baltimore

There's an oriole at my window,
his deep marigold body startling me
each time he lands to sip sugar water
from the orange feeder. Baltimore oriole,
not the American city or the baseball team,
but a bird named for the color of the coat of arms
of English nobleman Lord Baltimore who founded
the colony of Maryland and whose actual name
is Cecil W. Calvert—Calvert, name of the first

street I lived on, not in Baltimore but Detroit.
Though there is a Calvert Street in Baltimore where
a marble statue of Lady Baltimore, also known as
Baltimore's Statue of Liberty, was erected
September 12, 1822—also the date my husband
and I were married, but 1993.
                              Which brings me
to the Lady Baltimore Tearoom located, not
in Baltimore, but Charleston where Southern belle
Alicia Rhett Mayberry served novelist Owen Wister
a slice of the acclaimed Lady Baltimore cake
she's rumored to have created, though history
speculates the recipe actually belonged to sisters
Florrie and Nina Ottolenghi.
                              Wister, who had
the sweet tooth of an oriole, loved the cake
enough to write a romantic novel titled
Lady Baltimore about a soon to be married
groom who orders a Lady Baltimore wedding cake
not in Baltimore but Kingsport, and winds up
falling in love with the woman who takes
the order, marrying her instead.
                              No one knows
why the white cake with a boozy dried
fruit-and-nut filling crowned with swirls
of not orange but fluffy white frosting is called
Lady Baltimore cake.

Wister has a literary journal
named for him, nowhere near Baltimore, rather
Wyoming where I, who still call Michigan home,
won a prize for a poem I wrote, not about an oriole
but a raven, also the name of a football team,
the Baltimore Ravens, named after Poe, who was
born in Boston but buried at Westminster Hall,
located in Baltimore.

The Philosophical Nature of Peeps

Nested, attached, fused in symbiotic
harmony—gooey quintets of flat-
bottomed puffs—
                            there are no singular
Peeps, no loners—always packaged
in flocked procession.
                            Note their
resistance to being pulled apart,
how their skin crusts like sugared armor.

Is it preservatives or preservation
that allows them to retain those resolute
postures—hold their tiny dip-dot gaze?

Were Peeps philosophers they'd be
the Stoics, were they saints,
the Joan of Arcs, accepting life's

vicissitudes as part of their
collective destiny.
                            Once I realized

these marigold chicks could
transcend their confectionary
contours, I bloomed them

in the microwave, roasted them
into gelatinous oneness,
the caramel scent of sugar

wafting as they sank into amorphous
puddle—no screams, no wicked witch
melting on yellow road.

Left exposed, they become that road,
hard as brick—yet still desired
despite their stalwart staleness.

An Unkindness of Ravens

One flew into a poet's house and stayed—
seemed to prefer the company of men
to migratory winged things. Eventually
the man grew uneasy with his Poe-like

companion, the dark symbolism, the bird's
scavenging nature—so he lured it into a cage,
released it back to the wild. Through the window
he saw other ravens fly down, attack.

A flock is called *an unkindness of ravens*,
named for the mother pushing her young
from the nest forcing them to fly, survive.

It's said we choose our partners to relive
troubled childhoods, those who possess
familiar, even cruel traits—that we may change
the outcome and prove our worth.

The raven is bulky yet acrobatic—
can soar like eagles and owls.
You've heard its piercing bray
from high trees and jagged cliffs.

You don't want one in your home.
There are things in nature that can't be tamed,
the instinct for survival or a predator
with a hunger you can't satisfy.

When the Heart Needs a Stunt Double

When my mother said the word *divorce*
in response to my asking where my father
was—after she'd said, *he won't be back,*
I asked what the word meant, because
the closest association I could make to divorce
was *diving horse,* an image to make sense
of fairy-tale magic plunging from its own

dead weight. That day, having come home
from school where my father usually
asked what I'd learned—I learned
I knew little, me bedside, she
propped by pillows, reading a book—
barely looking up when she said,
It means he's never coming back.

I remember the whirl of confusion,
as if I'd heard a story read too fast
to comprehend its meaning—trying
to figure out how my father could
make such an exit with no goodbye,
the way a child might wonder how
the horse climbed so high
to take its spectacular dive.

My Drowned Lover's Soul Inhabits My Dog

I dream of Todd, of touching
his wool jacket and it feels
like my dog. I tell him
I love him. I say it freely,

easily, the way I tell my dog.
He looks through me, doesn't speak,
his blue eyes filled with the sea.

Along the shore a picket fence leans.
Windblown, it no longer separates
land and water, only earth and sky.

I turn to the water, tell it there is
something wrong with that fence,
the way it keeps its ear to the sand.

The fence replies, *I am still a fence—*
but one that no longer takes sides.

Some say our souls lose their
boundaries when we die,
free to become footprints
that come and go.

I look into the water's eye,
blue as the eye of my dog,
and realize the wave repeats
what it hears.
                    I say, *stay.*

Morning, I rise to sounds
of ball games in my yard.
I slip into a white silk robe,
study myself in the mirror.

I seem a stranger, but not
to my dog, never to my dog.

Come, I say. *Come inside.*

Close

When NPR announced Mars
will appear larger in the sky tonight,
that its orbit will bring it closer

to Earth, I thought of the times I've heard
you can almost touch it,
the misses and near misses,

the lingering before *yes* or *no*—
marriages, children, flights
that could have gone either way.

I thought of the trajectory
of roots of old trees, patches of land
inhabited by families

over centuries—the silent
march of footprints.
And the word *belonging*

how the towering pines in our yard
belong to us—used to
belong to someone else,

and will belong to others
who will claim them as their own—
I thought of the words

when we are gone
how we travel among our own
swath of humanity,

share the same moon,
see the same statues fall,
the same leaders rise.

Years ago, my husband showed me
Mars through his telescope—
stars and planets I'd never seen

simply because I never looked—
an unfathomable wilderness
that made me feel safer

just knowing there was more.
The news that followed Mars
was of the demise of a small boat

crammed with five hundred
human beings, their weight,
the weight of their longing

too heavy for the Saran of salt water
stretched to hold the words:
sistermotherfatherbrotherbabydaughterson.

With no space between them
they became one word, *refugees*,
unable to realize the dream

they could almost touch.
Now, I'm thinking about the difference
between night and day

how day is being
and night is searching—
and the sky—all that room.

Refugee

A house
without walls,
road that narrows
and snakes,
the haystack
backs that bear
the weight of steel-
cold nights,
the moon
cutting a portal
in the deserted
sky—view
black as a turtle's back.
It's a mouth's dark cave
liberating an eclipse
of white moths,
a shoal of footprints
swimming in sand
that disappears
beneath more sand,
the road erased
behind you,
eyes that follow
a flight of swallows
any direction
every direction
but home.

You Say the Kitchen Is Your Country

after Jane Hirshfield, for my Grandmother, Sittu

In your kitchen where parsley
was washed, the scent lingers

as earth must hold for a long time
the verdant scent of grass.

In a stainless basin,
the current gathers
clouds of sand, rinse of rain—

Lebanese cedar,
Mediterranean waters.

     *

Yes, I'm a Michigan girl
of lush peninsula, lake fed,

one who, you say, shares your blood
but not your soil.

Yet, in my kitchen where parsley is washed,
the parsley scent lingers

as one who's held your apron
knows the deep smell of your hands.

     *

Parsley—sweet *baqdounes*
sprig and fringe rising,
tabouli salad, *ihjee* omelet,

did I invite you in
with thoughts of unfenced gardens?

As one who straddles the gate
between our green oases—

as hunger migrates on massive wings,
and circles
between home and home.

Figaro Speaks

When our dog Figaro arrives home from his two-week boarding
at Maple Orchard Animal Clinic, he's vociferous—yelping,
chattering like a human in group therapy who'd been waiting
a *long* time to share. He circles us to make his points and *grrrs*
every once in a while. "Well, the food was fine, it's the same,
but there were all kinds of people and dogs, dogs I've never seen—
and I was often confined to a crate! I outgrew that crate
years ago, and well you weren't there to sing to me the way you do.
Another woman tried but it wasn't the same, and the songs were different
except for the one that goes *Figaro Figaro Figaro*. I tried to tell her you say
good morning and good night with a melody—that *I'm* the good boy,
but she just didn't get it. And the other dogs, some barked and yapped
for hours, others just sat there, dispassionate and bored. This is not
what I am accustomed to *grrr*. Not at all! I'm a creature of habit.
And well, this was amusing for a day or two but then it got rough,
ruff, ruff, ruff, ruff, ruff! Grrr, where's my treat? I need a treat."

Palm Reading Detroit

Michigan's forested hand,
verdant fingertips,
pines on periphery,
Montmorency cherry
cabin and thicket,
walleye, antlers
lighthouse and dune
Traverse City moon
tempers the lake
its glinting shimmer
won't smooth
this jagged line,
my restless shores.

Pour me a Stroh's,
I'm heading back
to Detroit, beaux arts
and deco, falcon
and ledge, tunnel
and bridge. Give me
Brown-Bomber Fist,
spoke and hub,
river and strait,
this rhythmic
skyline
read—love,
lifeline, home.

The Fist on Jefferson Avenue Meets Isaac Newton

Drive down Jefferson near the banks
of the Detroit River, you can't miss the massive

24-foot-long, 8,000-pound sculpture, a forearm
that cuts through the urban landscape

clean as the knockout Joe Louis delivered
to Max Schmeling. Dubbed *The Fist*, this "Monument

to Louis" might have taught Newton a thing or two.
Imagine pulling back the sleek bronze arm

to launch an unstoppable forward motion,
a hook, a cross, uppercut combos coming at you

again and again. His fists, fastest in history,
traveled mere inches ending in paralyzing explosions

His moves, efficient, accurate.
                              I've seen Joe's hands,
felt the warmth of his grip when I stood up with him
at a friend's Vegas wedding. Dressed in elegant white

he spoke with a soft tenor, had the searching eyes
of a four-year-old who lost his father, someone

ready to lend a hand, give away all his cash
even when it meant living in poverty.

I wish I'd talked to him more, but I was young,
ready to waste perfectly good moments, believing

like a pendulum, they'd return. Suspended in
a pyramidal frame, the massive Fist never sways

but it does set the mind in motion. Some say
it looks cocked, an in-your-face jab—head-on

like a truck rolling off the Rouge, others see it
as protective, ready to defend this city

that has taken its share of blows.

My Mother Cuts Me Open and Finds an Apple Inside

I swallowed it whole,
   a shiny red orb
to catch my mother's eye.

It slipped through my carotid
   like the moon
in Bashō's lake,

glided through my lungs—
   a luge
sledding on air.

It fell à la Newton's
   gravity into the cavity
of my heart,

rolled pinball smooth
   through channels
of vein and artery.

It bobbed like dashboard dolls,
   floating
on waves of plasma,

traversed my liver's lobes
   like Mallory
scaling Everest.

It swung across my pancreas—
   think Foucault's
leaded pendulum.

and slid through my intestines
   like Williams
sweet cold plum.

It bumper car-ed my ovaries
        dropping eggs
like ripe persimmons,

to be plucked
        by Mother's hand
who held it to the light,

and still
        didn't know me
any better.

Anatomy Lessons

1. Anatomy of the Body

If I hadn't worked for a doctor, I wouldn't have helped
suture a girl who fell through a glass window, arm flayed,
ulna exposed elbow to wrist. None of the office nurses
had the stomach for it. So, when he approached the reception
desk to ask if I could handle it, my answer was my promotion.
From then on, I helped excise sebaceous cysts, plantar warts,
assisted with Pap smears, administered injections: allergy,
hormone, baby vaccines. There were the pre and postnatal
checkups when I lifted infants firmly, held them confidently
to make them feel secure . . . And emergencies: removing
hardened hot lead from a man's face and lashes, or whispering
you're going to be alright in a man's ear while applying pressure
to his lacerated jugular. I can't forget trying to comfort a grieving
woman; the sight of her sons dragging her limp body through
the door. The loss of her beloved poodle took the life out of
her legs. I couldn't relate until 30 years later the weight
of sorrow took me down when my Westie died.

2. Anatomy of the Mind

If I hadn't responded to Sister Theresa, who during an interview
asked if I was Catholic, with, *No, but I have a good friend who is*,
I would not have been the only non-Catholic hired to work
for the Daughters of Divine Providence, a strict order of nuns
at Our Lady of Providence School. Might have missed the chance
to counsel ten-year-old abused girls and those with autism or Down
syndrome. I was the first to discover Diane suffered from a split
personality after listening to her speak in two distinct voices.
The submissive left side of Diane's body bruised by *Diana's*
punishing right fist. What if I never grew close to Andrea who often
drew human stick figures crouched inside a circle? Would she have
been coaxed into revealing the circle was the door of the clothes dryer
her mother stuffed her in for being a "bad girl"? And, I'd never have
known Marie, fourteen-year-old "bird girl," tiny as a six-year-old—
contorted features, webbed feet, speech so nasal she was barely
understood. No one noticed her interest in the musculoskeletal system.
She'd found an old anatomy book, showed it to me day after day,
pointing out the ulna, wrist, elbow—pressing mine. I let her explore

my face, my skull. She knew every bone in the human body, told me
she was going to be a doctor—and that she knew she wasn't pretty.

3. Anatomy of the Soul
If I hadn't developed agoraphobia from a wounding childhood,
I would not have given up my counseling job to open an art gallery
close to home—my psych degree useful for exploring nuances, themes
in works such as Munch's *Scream*, self-portrait of a tormented man frozen
beneath a shrieking sky. His anguish stirred by the scarring loss of his mother
and sister, at the tender age of five. I lifted the veil of Magritte's Lovers,
couple kissing through shrouded cloth, inspired by young Magritte's
gruesome discovery, mother's body washed up on shore, nightgown
coiled, covering her head. It was no surprise to learn the distorted faces
of Picasso's *Weeping Woman* were born of cruelty toward his lovers,
or how the influence of angular African masks on Cubism became symbols
of his misogyny. More disturbing, the pleasure he took in wounding them.
I studied wartime model/photographer Lee Miller, damaged by her father
who photographed her, age seven through her twenties, nude. Flashes
that illuminate her somber admission of a knack for distance "in matters
of sentiment." The camera lens, a stoic boundary between her and horrific
piles of skeletal remains stacked like firewood at Buchenwald, the starved
glass-eyed prisoners "waiting" at Dachau. And Frida Kahlo who suffered
a broken spine along with a broken heart when she learned through
a portrait on Rivera's mural of his affair with her beloved sister.
Her self-portrait, *Two Fridas*, one traditional the other modern—past
and present holding hands, their visible hearts exposed beneath a roiling
sky. I found such poetry in Goya's *Saturn Devouring His Son*. Saturn,
fearing he'd be overthrown by his children, ate each one at birth. Perhaps
a metaphor—devour the anguish before it devours you.

Planetary Biology at Beaumont Hospital

They wilted the tulips out of me—the needles,
taps, surgeries, and tests like transesophageal
echocardiograms with scopes the size of satellites,
that must be swallowed.
                                    Somewhere in the mitral, aortic,
pulmonary valves, the doctors look for vegetation—
life on Mars. If our organs had planetary names,
the heart would have to be Mars. And the vegetation:

alpha hemolytic streptococcus, bacterial endocarditis,
septicemia, with microbes that bloom pretty as loosestrife—
the Eurasian perennial that chokes out native flowers,
same way exotic trees planted in foreign soil drink
the river dry.
                        Seems I have a flair for the extraterrestrial,
have invited alien cells to party hearty on this host before:
good old *Entamoeba histolytica,* dysentery contracted
on a trip to Algeria. And later, an exotic yogurt drink imported
the Hells Angels of bacteria to mess with microflora
in my colon—drove the nerdy good guys out.
                                                            And though
I no longer drink the tap water in Acapulco or eat hot dogs
from vendor carts, these bacterial blossoms sense
my immune system has a weakness for the bad guys—

all spiffed up in loosestrife purple and tulip-red—
ready to dance on a glass-slide stage beneath
the luminous lens of a microscope.

Anesthesia Awareness

Dreams morph to nightmares
lying on the operating table
she seems lifeless
under anesthesia
but her brain is not asleep
her body cold, paralyzed
she can't speak
can't move to let them know
she's awake, can hear
everything being said
cutting, pulling, tugging
the feral pain
her lungs powerless
a song without words
the strong narcotic
a way to control, to numb

for an unattended child
assumed to be unaware, oblivious
as a stuffed poodle, rubber doll
in a state of unconsciousness
someone gives her a comb, a coat
no one gives her kisses
no one considers the words of a girl
in a patriarchal culture
"females have no voice"
becomes part of her consciousness
mingling with shame
she tries to diminish
someone gave her life, a heart
big enough for love
they lied about
"you won't feel a thing."

Ya'aburnee

Arabic: "May you bury me." Term of endearment expressing the wish to die before your loved one rather than live without them.

Habibi: my love.
Hayete: my life.
Ward albi: rose of my heart.

What word means
to breathe in greedily,
overcome by the scent of a rose?

Shahwa: desire—
scent that moves
through your feet,
turns the soil.

Shafaf: Diaphanous, ethereal, vague—
everything but your name.

How do you say, love in spite of fear?

Shawka: thorn
to realize
it is the thorns
that have roses.

Tuq: yearning—
when petals have withered,
and the memory of perfume
settles inside you like stones.

How much would you have to love someone
to bury them?

Ya Amri: my life.
Ya Rouhi: my soul.

Il hubb: love—
weight that lifts you
and buries you at once.

Excuses for Not Falling in Love

My heart wears the hide of Spanish bulls.

    My feet are two grifters on the make.

My mind rides a luge on icy hills.

    My kiss is a rare night-blooming orchid.

My hope flickers like old neon signs.

    My eyes are Duchamp's nude, descending.

My heart's built of tempered glass and mortar.

    My fear is the mouth of Jeita Grotto.

My eyes are the arctic fox that wanders.

    My tongue memorizes rules of sweetness.

My nose follows smoke and wild dogs.

    My lips like to ransack and to plunder.

My heart is tattooed with skull and crossbones.

    My ears take their cues from rolling stones.

My eyes are the gates of horn and ivory.

    My mind is the Gordian undone.

My limbs are the arms of Bruegel's *Beggars*.

    My soul makes its living off of duende.

My heart is the ship that leaves the bottle.

My Eyes Find the Face of the Person I Love
and Pull Out Their Fork and Knife

He toyed with his spoon, then mine, then with the knives, the forks,
so enchanted by what had first compelled him.
How easily love and food are confused.
Before, ache never seemed long like a tunnel,
it was a cri de coeur
ready to consume half of everything it gives.
Then it was inside the tree, the rock—the cloud
I let drink rain from the pulse of my throat.

Sometimes I still put my hand tenderly on my heart
when one clock hand embraced the other,
put my minutes there, on you, as hands—touch, press,
hosing my nostrils with fragrance
like cinnamon coaxed back out of the tongue.

This morning I stepped outside and the blue nearly crushed me,
as if it were reading the earth with its blind shadow.
When I thought it was right to name my desires
because nothing is truly forgotten *and* loved,
my voice went into the nowhere, into the hard, black ear—
a red bird who caught fire on the alchemist's table.

But I who want to smoke and make mirages
with a cardboard guitar, a map of the planets,
weave a darkness plush as mole fur with my tongue.
I turned back to the animal. No, it turned its back to me
and left you bruised and ruined, you poor sad thing.
Why must we be so intent on destroying everything we touch?

Title: Ruth Madievsky, "Electrons"
1. Carol Ann Duffy, "Mrs. Midas"
2. Mark Doty, "What Is the Grass"
3. Tung-Hui Hu, "The Wish Answered"
4. Curtis Bauer, "Self Portrait in Dark Interior"
5. C. D. Wright, "One with Others"
6. Geffrey Davis, "King County Metro"
7. Jane Hirshfield, "First Light Edging Cirrus"
8. Kim Addonizio, "Muse"
9. Alicia Ostriker, "Ghazal: America the Beautiful"
10. Perry Janes, "Notes on Discovery: Dismantling a Clock"
11. Jorie Graham, "Reading to My Father"
12. Norman Dubie, "Trombone"
13. Donald Dunbar, "Clonazepam"

Neruda in My Kitchen

Think pie. Tender pastry
anointed with golden moons
of butter, ethereal crust
filled with cherries the color
of a savage harvest,
                              its scent,
prey for the crazed puma
prowling the hollow street
of your hunger.
                    Luminous
slice—a sonnet written
in stains of crimson,
nectars of cerise.
                        Let each bite
linger on your tongue—
flowering stars pulsing
with red laughter.
                        Because
my darling, when the pie
is gone you will miss it the way
a lonely house would miss
its only window. Repeat,

I pace around hungry,
sniffing the twilight,
hunting for you,
for your hot molten heart.

The Strange Fate of Falling into a Black Hole

in response to an untitled sketch by Edward Marsh

They say it could happen to anyone,
you're out for a walk, starless black
night, when you find yourself
burrowing a hole into the fabric
of reality, spinning
until you're   split in two.

One you, a loyal Venus who
never ventures far from the sun
                now plunging through
love's feathery darkness,
your body tattooed
        with all the kisses you've ever been given.

The other, flighty firebird
prone to bursts of lust,
        your particulates smoldering
into a sooty swath of crows.

And because
        nothing is black and white
            you must color the word
        that means *hunger,*

your mannered appetite
for everyone and everything
an open mouth
            where crows return
the enigma of your wholeness,

their wings now your wings
resembling the angel
you never were,
and never will be.

In the Garden of the Universe

When the physicist said every piece of everyone—everything
you look at, from the thing you hate to that which is most precious,
was assembled by forces of nature in the first moments
of the universe—it took the artist back to her earliest memory
of being one with the soil.

> A packet of wildflowers
> spills willy-nilly
> hard to decipher the weeds

Imagine what she might have written in her journal—
At night my dandelions evoke the grace of prayer.
They fold their florets like evening primrose
having gathered the moon and the scattered stars.

> Dearest—wise old confessor
> my secrets lie in
> your seeded beard unfolding

The physicist said when you die pieces of you will return
to the universe in the endless cycle of death and rebirth.
The artist understood this when she carved *Viva la Vida*
into the fruit of her last work, a still life of watermelons,
whole and hewn against an open blue sky.

Later her husband, the famed muralist, by coincidence
or affinity, assembled a lush tableau—watermelons,
his final painting—flesh pulsing ripe and red,
sown with glossy black seeds.

> Inside every seed and leaf
> viva la vida
> this is where you will find me

"I Feel Like I Sprained My Damn Heart"

—Whitey Winn, *Godless*

It happens—not the moment
your lover says it's over, before
your heart limps like a wounded
animal, before you sink into the shelter
of your own shadow realizing
you're no longer afraid of anything,
not even the dark.
                    Rather it happens
when you think the ache has faded
and you find yourself noticing
the last crimson leaf unsling
from a stark branch, its slow sway
and soft landing—so light, so brittle
that when you touch it, it all falls apart.

Extirpation

An expired packet of wildflower seeds found
in a drawer reminds me I have a habit of resisting love,
I name it possibility and forget what that means—

a habit of unearthing the past that taught me
to get used to the leaving before the leaving—
though it may never come.

I'm a damn fool and I know it.
What good does it do to learn
sadness before sadness teaches
its weighty lessons? We live in a land

of endangered species: prairie trillium,
marsh violet, rock jasmine, and beaked agrimony.

My astrological flower, the morning glory,
says this is how I'm supposed to flourish:
You bloom beautifully right where you are planted—

in the green of my Midwest yard, not the desert
where venomous scorpions dwell: the deathstalker,
the emperor, the man-killer fattail—

Transplant a tree from a wet climate to a dry one,
it will drink the riverbeds dry. Transplant
a heart using the venom of a scorpion,
it will increase its chance of survival.

Whoever chose to try it first is braver than I.
Yet, comforting to know, when hearts fail here,
they'll thrive somewhere else.

Heartbreak Number One

Your finger, its flesh cocoons a sliver—splinter
from a sheltering tree. To remove it would ache, to keep it,
would ache like the smooth veneer that betrayed you.
This wound needs your attention, will redden its lips,

weep its sap, interrogate until your finger wags
its broken compass, finds solace in the cooling air.
Oak maple willow elm, limbs reaching beyond
your homey yard to sprawl in tangled wilderness.

How exquisite, how delicate our sense of touch,
and how we are touched by what is broken.
This tree—its roots coil your finger
to remind you certain kisses will scar.

Heat is strong. Pain is strong. Passion is strong.
And now everything strong leaves you weak.

Tatterdemalion

The legend of Tatterdemalion: a child banished to live in the woods who will
make you love him only to steal your health.

Because the forest is not made of light,
and the rhythmic procession
of twigs snapping is enough
to sound like life breaking—

the feral child appeals to your sense
of hunger and begs for sweetness,
the dupe of swapping your candy
for his salt. And before you know it,

he invites you to his woodlands
to show you how soil provides
the roots with anchorage,
which you take as a wish for connection

until the knowing eye sees through the child,
witnesses the flowering of decay
as you gaze at your reflection in a still pond,

the spectacle of your red hair turning white,
a tree in autumn shedding every last leaf,
its barren arms forever open.

Snow Falls Off Bare Branch

At a reading, the poet responds to the art
of the Japanese woodblock. But I only see
the back of the man's head blocking my view,

white hair combed counterclockwise, hiding
terrain where grass no longer grows—
the pale heart of a lone chrysanthemum.

As the poet cites Hiroshige's cobalt skies,
the mum becomes a lotus on the bald pond
at Shinobu. By the time she references

Wild Geese Flying Across a Crescent Moon,
I migrate to the edge of my seat,
glimpse the side of his face. Hair parted

at the temple, it swoops his forehead—
Hokusai's *Great Wave*. The poet shows
thirty-six views of Mt. Fuji, I see but one,

barren land between distant mountain
and shrouded roof. When she recites haikus
for the four seasons. I hear winter:

> Snow covered pine bough
> holds promise of green until
> a gust shakes it bare.

The Art of Kintsugi

The Japanese art of repairing broken pottery with gold dusted lacquer to highlight rather than hide its fractures. Also known as art of precious scars. / For Per Wierup.

To make the repair
the surgeon
must fracture
the sternum
east west

he must think in halves
to spread the ribs
right left
and then consider what is right
what is left

he must palpate
the jagged edges of loneliness.

> Once I dated a guy
> it was snowing
> there was a concert
> we were to go together
> words drove us apart
>
> when he ran to his car
> sped off
> I ran after him
> my hands clamped
> to the bumper
> feet sliding in snow,
> the zigzag
> of tracks, my EKG,
> before letting go.

In order for the surgeon
to find the wound
he must feel
the muscle
that builds the walls
that have grown too thick

observe
how hard the muscle
has worked
lifting and lowering
the weight of love and sorrow.

To make the repair
the surgeon must admire
the beauty of wholeness,
cobble and collage,

in order to form
the gilded scar
that marries
the sides,
smooths the edges.

What Saves Her

A woman I've just met tells me she swims 120 laps an hour,
three days a week. Says she's learned to control her body—

graceful arcs, breathing from the diaphragm, filling it
with pink air. *Your lungs go down to here* she says,

scanning the top of her rib cage to her noticeably trim waist.
If you're going to have to live, you might as well feel good—

her body defined, strong——cultivated beauty born
of discipline that makes not the routine of swimming

but the chore of living worthwhile. And though I want
to know more, I decide to tread, take her at the surface

she seems to value so much. Later I learn she was broken
over her divorce, that honing her physique

is a recent obsession. A friend once argued
it's not beauty's job to save us, though I have

been saved by it—my pen surfing the blank page,
traveling beyond spoken language. Intimate layers

falling away to reveal just how naked I can be.
Once, it allowed me to relive the day I almost

drowned, my body, panicked, flailing, desperate
to hold on to life's massive lung—the fear

of never knowing what more I could be. For some,
beauty comes naturally, others work hard

for its allure of happiness. Maybe it's true
beauty cannot save us, when I think of how quickly,

how quietly one can drown in it, our gaping
mouth taking it in as it swallows us whole

The Girl from Ipanema Visits Detroit, 1964

Slender, exotic—a jazz singer with smooth dark hair,
Adele arrived from Malone, New York, where she
and my mother grew up. Here to perform at Baker's,

she never knew her brief stay was enough that I at thirteen
would shelve the Motown sounds of Junior Walker,
and Gladys Knight for all that jazz. The only

jazz I'd listened to was Getz and Gilberto
because "The Girl from Ipanema" was #5 on the charts.
After Adele left, I stood at the mirror, singing

tall and tan and young and lovely . . . bought
Brubeck's *Take Five*, Montgomery's guitar riffs,
hoping her sleek sophistication would glide

through me like the silky notes of Smokey
and Marvin. I eyed the cool loungy
demeanor that, for her, came easy as Ella

though I had no clue what I'd do with it. What I knew
was even in black stirrups, turtleneck, and curly hair
smoothed slick, my reflection rang dissonant as those

jazz instrumentals I tried so hard to like—I didn't exude
the aloof, bossa nova vibe of *when she passes*
each one she passes goes aaaah. Like other girls

in my neighborhood, I wasn't groomed to follow
my passions or even know what they were, needed
lyrics with r-e-s-p-e-c-t to tell me what to want.

Soon, jazz just didn't jive. It lacked the soul
of "My Girl," the cool new beat of "Dancing in the Street"
and I'd had enough syncopated improvisation,

collecting bits and pieces of others to collage myself
whole. Back then, if Adele had asked what I want,
I would have said the wonder of Stevie, the marvel

of Marvelettes, the Dee-troit strut of Temps and Tops—
voices that would drown out Gilberto's ethereal
whispers in a song that was never about the girl

but about a lonely guy who could only watch
this ephemeral beauty *swing so cool and sway so gently*—
a girl, unattainable, even to herself.

Instructions for the Aspiring Rock Star, Circa 1894

Stride out from the wings of your Neo-Renaissance concert hall
and saddle up to ride all that is Franz Liszt—handsome, exotic
rock star virtuoso with a rhapsodic vibe. Ease yourself
onto the bench of your solid silver piano, hold a dramatic pause,
then finger those ivories with the smooth melodic grace notes

of gypsy folk songs, gradually building to lightning fast
yet graceful frenzy adding risky thunderous leaps, trills,
arpeggios with rapid chord changes while whipping your head
like an ocean current, long hair flying, sweat beads glistening—
you'll barely notice the dissonant ululations of corseted women

who've by now flouted all rules of decorum as you unsheathe
your green silk glove, one elegant finger at a time, before tossing it
with the flair of, well, *Liszt*, into a female frisson of adoration.
Some will faint, others swoon and rush the stage to tear off
tiny bits of your frock coat—their screams reverberating

all the way to the dawn of Elvis. Lisztomaniacs pinned
with cameos of your portrait, yanking locks of your wild hair.
Cultured countesses brawling over broken piano strings
they'll fashion into bracelets. After the concert enjoy a cigar.
A good one. You can afford it. You're a rock star. Men envy you,

women want to bed you. Now, toss the butt into the gutter
only to catch sight of a woman tucking it into her cleavage
that she may encase in a locket adorned with your diamond
initials. Don't be surprised when even your coffee dregs
are preserved in vials to be worn as precious jewels.

Wild Spirit

Carbon, from Latin *carbo*, it's the element
that bonds to form numerous chemical
and biological molecules: graphite, coal,
diamonds—sun, stars, comets.

Colorless, odorless, it leaves footprints
of our impact on the planet, cycles between
air and water as carbon dioxide with an almost
James Bond nomenclature: CO_2, Atomic #6.
Essential to the daisies it forms with our every
breath, fizzes our Perrier, propels our aerosols.

Discovered as *a substance distinct from air*
after a chemist observed a shrunken mass
of charcoal burned in a closed vessel. His theory:
the rest became invisible gas or *wild spirit*.

Carbon is what we are made of, who we are.
It's also what we can be. Consider Life Gems,
a business that captures that wild spirit,
turning mortal remains into diamonds. Their theory:
We're made from carbon, diamonds are made
of carbon, if somehow, you're able to combine
the two, you'll have a beautiful memorial.

Ashes to ashes, dust to diamonds—carbon,
from the remains of cremated loved ones—
a special bond in the form of a ¼ to 1¼ carat
sparkling gem. One client who lost his daughter
described the stone as *having a lot of fire,*
personality and character, like Valerie.

Unlike the starting bond a friend forged with his
mother the night he drove to their cottage
to scatter her ashes on the lake. He stopped at a bar,
got weepy drunk, and told a stunned woman his mother
was in the trunk. Later, he rowed out to the middle
of the lake, threw the urn over, but it wouldn't sink,
just kept following him.

Though not for everyone,
prehistoric carbon with naturally occurring allotropes
lets your loved one continue to shine. Atom to molecule,
pendant to chain—diamonds really are forever.

Pareidolia Speaks

I wander, a hungry shadow,
emerge as Jesus on a flour tortilla,
the Virgin Mary framed inside the crust
of a grilled cheese sandwich.

I'm the pasta that stuck
to the plate forming
the word *Papa*,
after your father died,

the silhouette scissored
from shades of night—
Sasquatch in the forest,
Loch Ness, elephant
rock in Iceland.

Or the Rorschach that teases
you with a bat, a crab?
I'm the dead wife you run to,
until you realize I'm not.

The face you want
to forget, the one
you almost forgot,

the smile you see on
a parking meter,
butterfly on the MRI,

man in the moon
who smiles
and disappears,
smiles and disappears—

I am the lost and found.

Electric Metamorphosis

after Electric Caterpillar sculpture by Sabine Meyer Zu Reckendorf

Yes, I could hang upside down all day
banging out the shiny chrysalis—
winged cape intricate as Persian rugs,

but these imaginal cells
that let me shape my destiny
are too big to be constrained,
restrained.
              No, my wings
are celestial—less Icarus, more
Star Trek, unfolding stipple and dot,
a conflagration of stars that say,
I will find you in the dark with

my lovely appendage-*ment*—
these Skittles-colored legs
transparent as Lucite. Come,

explore my nocturnal side,
where the sky meets the mettle.

My fibers are optic.

Three Stages of Abandonment

1-Youth
>She spent hours pacing the Persian rug,
tracing intricate lines of spiraling leafy
>>branches with tips that split to jaws
of a dragon. When she closed her eyes
>>the carpet hovered, its silk fringe
like tattered wings of an owl, lifting her

>>above the ordinary living room
to wondrous spheres where glasswing
>>butterflies migrate among flowers
lucent as glass. A place where vein and stalk
>>have no secrets.

2-Adolescence
>Her home was divided by exotic scents,
perfume and pipe tobacco. To the west, mother,
>>the east, the ghost of absent father who said
"Transparency has little to do with seeing,"

>>which she decoded as memory is a gift
of one's own making. And so, it was normal,
>>to be the young Arabian princess
with her fine Arabian horse and her red
>>velvet pouch of exotic sweets.

3-Maturity
>She traced a heart that flourished
from a brain to a bird that fancied itself heart's
>>companion—before she realized mind and heart
split like reason and wanting. That's when it became clear
>>a Persian rug, like all rugs, tends toward
gravity, having absorbed the weight
>>of footsteps—the coming, the going.

Open Heart Surgery

for Per Wierup

I've had it once before,
         when father left.
Heart fell onto the floor, red
         as a Cetti's warbler egg,

leaving a crack
         I hadn't fathomed
would invite sounds
         of light and dark.

I picked it up, held it
         the way a birder
might rescue a fledgling—
         became drawn to men
partial to damage—
         not wound, more
artful nest that hides it,

         learned how to plug
lachrymal effusions
         near bones tiny
as the breast of a weebill.

         All ornithologists
should study the ear,
         the shaded nuances
of the auditor ossicles
         in order to discern
the most subtle chirps.

Most have listened
to the *thump thump thump*
     of this pulse unseen
but not all are capable
     of opening the cage
that cradles it.

     and few are capable of
opening the bird itself.

Saudade

after the painting "Separation" by artist Edvard Munch

Having glimpsed the one, a man holds his hand
over his heart to keep it from falling
from his chest. It has seared, burned through his suit.
Rivers, birds, clouds—everything has stopped
but longing that nourishes the earth at his feet. Rising
from the soil, a large crimson flower shaped

as . . . a couple's embrace? He turns away, is in no shape
to approach the woman behind him. Her hand
outstretched, she glides toward the sea, gold hair rising,
floating, even gravity can't keep her down. Crestfallen,
his mouth forms an empty O. He knows he must stop
hoping—that she won't return. Who hasn't felt unsuited

for the risk of attachment? Closets filled with suits
of mourning. The loss of lovers, friends, shaping,
coloring us dark as Demeter's unstoppable
grief. The man indulges his desire. On one hand,
the ache but also the haunting memory of falling
in love. Dear Munch, you who reprise

saudade, the homesick rush of nostalgia rising—
bittersweet scent of a dying rose. Your pursuit
of mood bruising the canopy of sky, nightfall's
dark alchemy turning Rorschach blots to shapes
of remote islands. And what about his hand
outlined with the red of his lovesick heart? She stops

to offer a final glance. Or maybe she's stopped
because she isn't real—an ethereal spirit rising,
haunting reminder for one unable to handle
another loss. The woman breezes by, brushing his suit.
His head bowed beneath black leaves shaped
like footprints disappearing into the wistful aura of fall.

But what if I'm wrong? What if he's fallen
in love with melancholy itself, a habit he can't stop
revisiting? Her dress forms a loose-shaped
heart unable to stand on its own. So, no surprise
it lies on its side, plays dead. His pursuit,
a withered fate slipping through his hands.

Sorrow reshapes the seasons. He rises
to fall, yet still that tug of spring which suits
this dystopian palette, this love he can't unhand.

A Taste for Duende

ars poetica

Lie in the cool night grass
that bends to your will and tilt
toward flash and speck, where planets
tease and nymphs ignite Lorca's
secret and shuddering, his
ghost and glimmer.

And should you find yourself
skygazing with someone lost,
point to a world named after them,
untethered. Watch it become
itself: glossy, elusive with the specter
of darkness—for tension.

Know that if you say it you'll see it:
the shamrock spared from footprints
of the unlucky, woman at the souk
who hawks fabric woven of saudade

and the poet who desperately tries to feed
her shadow. When she names it
nourishment, duende corrects her,
names it *hunger*, names it *curse*.

Guilt Masquerades as Pleasure
at the Venetian Ball of Sweets

1- Guilt and Sin Strut Their Stuff
A plump biology teacher makes her grand entrance
Roman Catholic style. She wears a nun's tunic,
scapular and cowl covered in sequins that do little
to hide food stains dotting her ample chest. "I thought
I'd bring the divine back to divine providence," she says,
turning to the Unisons, a small Greek chorus. She carries
the new edition of *The Joy of Baking*, says it's her Bible.

A priest sidles up. "Your neighbors, the Giovannis complained
they can see into your kitchen. Your eating habits have made them fat."
"How is that possible?" chime the Unisons. "It isn't osmosis," Priest says,
"a study revealed when we dine with those who eat fast, we tend to eat faster.
When they take two helpings we follow like wayward flocks." "What can I do?"
asks the nun. "Virtue requires we know trial, suffering. Cannoli are laid
at our doorstep, and it is we who pluck the pome from the tree."
When asked where he gets his cannoli the priest says
he's partial to Randazzo's on Staten Island.

2- The Analyst Steps In
"We've all been baptized in the brine of shame. But drop a line into the ocean
of humanity and you'll find others ready to take the bait of your afflictions."

3- A Catholic Girl of Italian Descent Hears Our Confession
We, my accomplice Mondo and I, poison a man at his request, feeding him
ricotta cheesecake and hazelnut gelato IVs. We roll him into the back of our van,
drive to the farmers market and shop for broccoli rabe and cippolini onions, posing
as vegans rather than the sugar addicts we've become. A virgin farm girl spots us
and removes a red lollipop from the pocket of her jeans. She licks it feverishly, says
she has an affinity for sweets and winks. I take this as a sign to return the produce
and confess our crime. "It was a mercy killing," I plead. "I get it," she replies, removing
her burlap apron. She tells us she's tired of selling organic fennel and shouts, "*Andiamo
alla festa!*" We drive to the victim's home, though we're unprepared to confess our
deed to his wife. Instead, we tell her we are fruit leather reps. She asks to see what
we have, pushing us aside as she walks toward our minivan, and notices her husband's
gold Versace sneakers poking out of the lambswool we used to cover him up. She removes
the lilies hiding his face. "How did it happen?" she asks tearfully. We tell her he's been

clinically depressed since his diagnosis of adult onset diabetes. Rather than give up dessert he chose to die by elemental sucrose infusion. "I've known for some time," she says, "it's the way he wanted to go." The widow thanks us. "I couldn't have done it." She asks about the fruit leather, which we never had. "Do you have chocolate?" When we say no she seems irritated. We suspect she's been an enabler. She tells us to wait and returns with a pink feather duster fashioned as a Venetian mask for his wake. The rest of us dress as Venetian acrobats capable of somersaulting over tickly issues. But our costumes do little to disguise our mounting anxiety and lack of willpower. Even our lethargic dog Bobo seems nervous, sniffing our shoes obsessively. I whisper to my accomplices, "We are going straight to Hell." The widow overhears and slaps me. I ask her to slap me again.

4- The Analyst Chimes In
"In life as in dreams we are all the characters, play all the roles."

5- On to Games and a Minuet
"Here's how this goes," the game chaperone says, "I will begin a phrase, then you'll respond with a curtsy before completing it. Ready? Begin:"

"To the untrained eye . . ."
"The zircon looks as good as the diamond," says the socialite.
"To the untrained ear . . ."
"It won't register that most cars honk in the key of F," says the pianist.
To the untrained nose . . .
"It isn't obvious the apple is a member of the rose family," says the poet.
To the untrained mouth . . .
"It's surprising your lips find pleasure in the most unusual places," says the voluptuous baker.

6- Moment of Reflection with a Quote by Kerouac
Ma poi loro ballarono in giù le strade come dingledodies.

But then they danced down the streets like dingledodies,
and I shambled after as I've been doing all my life . . .
because the only people for me are the mad ones, the ones
who are mad to live, mad to talk, mad to be saved.

7- *Time to Sup*
The menu: A fifteen-layer rosewater cake with mousseline buttercream frosting.
"We'd better say *grazie a Dio*," says the priest.

"Without Thy presence, naught, O Lord, is sweet,
No pleasure to our lips can aught supply.
Whether 'tis wine we drink or food we eat,
or the sweet, sweet glitter that dusts our feet."

Sex, Guilt, and Counter Espionage, Sinatra Style

My man and I are moon bathing in the summer sea
when out of nowhere Grandma, dead twenty years, appears
like one of Dante's demons, I hide behind my guy
since Gram, a walking chastity belt, was never down
with naked, or sex, or even innuendo. But as always,

she cracks the code with her super wa-wa vision,
her eyes glomming onto gleaming droplets trickling
down my goosefleshed back. And oh, how easily
they spill, telling all babbling-brook style *"No place
to hide when you're naked as the shimmer of moonlight."*

They say our brains delete old memories,
but somehow this ghostly spy, this Druze dowager
I call Double O NO! has managed to hack into
my Catholic conscience even though I'm not Catholic.

So, I flee to an Ozark ice cave, and there she is again!
When I realize my pretense of studying the melting point
of stalactites affected by hot heavy breathing rings false—
I snap a giant icicle from the cave's ceiling only to discover

the phallic spears are no match for her icy stares.
Even dead, grandma, who once said she could see
me everywhere, including bathroom stalls at grade school,

has a way of breaching my resolve with her dragnet drama.
Luckily, my man, a Sinatra aficionado and self-proclaimed
buzzkill killer comes *blowin' in from across the sea.*

He lingers there to touch my hair and just like that,
she vanishes. So I grab his hand and do what anyone
fending off repression from a psychologically
damaging family member does: I cue the orchestra and then
we walk across the sand, my sweetheart
and the summer wind, the warm summer wind.

Solving for X

I looked at my father's face 365 days
× 7.5 years which = 2,737.5, multiplied
by 3 × a day—a nourishment. Now
I calculate the difference

between the size of my face, petite
constellation, and the mass of his,
on par with say, Canis Major,
the big dog.
            Subtract the years
I didn't see him which was infinitely >
the years I did. Factor in the posit:
anything higher than 0 degrees emits light,

even as the sum of his eyes + lips + nose
diminished like the syzygy of a solar eclipse.
I discover time + distance has left me
thinking of him far < I used to. Usually

when dark craters + bright highlands = man
in the moon, which occurs every 29.5 days
or roughly 12 × a year, which thus = x:
the quantifiable equation of separation.

My Grandfather My Madame X

In a photo, this man I'd only met once wears a luxurious
cashmere coat, the soft rolling pleats of a paisley silk scarf
belie his posture, erect as the ancient bronze *Orator*.
His hand grips an accordion briefcase with brass fittings
suggesting . . . an expansive mind? I analyze each detail

the way I study symbols in paintings—Sargent's
Madame X, the drapes and cinches of her black satin gown.
Her pale, stark flesh against an imposing brown background—
all glow and shadow, bodice revealing and concealing at once.

In another photo my grandfather presents a well-tailored suit,
classic striped tie—leather-bound notebook splayed over one
hand, fountain pen in the other. His gaze travels beyond
the frame, seems to ride an arc into the distant future where
I sit now. These portraits had currency in the 1880s, narrated
with garments and poses to reveal status, interests.

I'm more familiar with Virginie Amélie Avegno Gautreau
aka Madame X. Have studied the contrasts that heighten
her interior tension: muscular arm pressed against a mahogany
side table conveying inner strength, her other arm loose, fleshy
and feminine, her sensual long neck, provocative, exposed.

Unlike my grandfather's stiff posture, slight tilt of head,
three-quarter pose, arranged by the Portuguese photographer
whose name is stamped on the back. His stance reveals
little of his inner world. I turn to another photo, note his

attention to detail, the crisp fold of pocket silk and braided
tassled belt that match the muted plaid lapels of his robe.
His choice of ascot seems measured as the tassels that hang
evenly. The care that is taken. That might have been taken.

A style icon, Madame X fashioned her hair with a nod to
the Hellenic era. Her tiara's diamond crescent an allusion to Diana,
goddess of fertility, the hunt, the moon. A counterpoint to her bare
shoulders, and slender jeweled straps flaunting sex, and wealth,
along with the pseudonym, Madame XXX.

                        Grandfather, word rarely
uttered by me. I was fifteen and homesick when we met—my one
brief visit to Lebanon where I learned he spent a decade in Portugal
working in textiles, collaborating with noted fashion designers,
one who created the three elegant dresses my mother wore
for my parents' three-day wedding. And that he was unwavering
in his kindness to her, even after their divorce.

                        Grandfather, his embrace,
warm as lambswool. A contrast to the roughhewn cloth I wore inside,
heavy bolt of coarse indifference inspired by those who dressed me in it
after my father left. He was the stranger who knew how to soften me,
one who showed me the miracle of love at first sight. Cradling my face
in firm but gentle hands, he held his gaze with tenderness
that spoke to my most vulnerable self.

                        Sargent said a good portrait
leaves the viewer with more questions than answers. What else
did my grandfather hold dear? Will I ever unspool the threads
to weave, not cloth, but the fabric of his life?

My Colosseum

I was no virago leading a heroic revolt against the Roman Empire,
rather, determined to get my degree, I'd waged a battle against
panic disorder—invincible soldier undaunted by tonics, or words.

Steadfast, panic attacked twenty times a day, its army a procession
prodding me to the arena of agoraphobia—agora: marketplace,
and phobia, the lions set to devour as anticipation trumpets
anxiety's hasty arrival.
                              I felt powerless against adrenaline's chemical warfare,
surrendering to its dogged assault just months before graduating from
an urban university, days after a friend was murdered on campus.

Later, my analyst, a Freudian jouster, drove a spear through my shaky resolve,
declaring, *some people aren't cut out for college*—oblivious to the insult,
and my warrior inclinations.
                              Willing to sacrifice a year of hard-fought credits,
I chose another university in a college town, farther away. But phobias,
possessive as kings to kingdoms, tied me closer to home—a bite-sized campus
in the burbs. My armor, barely adequate, legs, an unsteady stead—

so wobbly there were days before graduation I crawled
through the halls, my knees buffing the slick, cold floors, eyes
fixated on the classroom door—distant as ancient Rome.

Military Secrets

Crouched under our mahogany table
I pull the dining chairs in tight. The curve
of cabriole legs forms a pageant of female
soldiers—my soldiers, instructed by me

to disguise themselves as the graceful bars
of a fanciful birdcage where the only visitors allowed
are homey scents of warm bread and broth
wafting from the kitchen. The aromas,

I tell my soldiers, are the secret weaponry
of our detachment. Scents dispatched to infiltrate
the unwitting—draw them in to surrender their hunger
to the illusion of affection.
                                        I've learned much
in my grandmother's kitchen, where the warmth
of the stove softens her, the way a slice of bread
softens hard stones of sugar.
                                        Through the bars I eye
the Corot above the buffet. A lone French peasant
woman in a landscape of pond and arbor where
in the lush green silence it's possible to discern voices
of a thousand men especially my father who forgot
to teach me how to survive captivity in the wild.

The woman's body reminds me of grandma,
the way the arch of her sturdy back
confronts the fertile fields she harvests.

Since our family became fractured, I've been
halted by the stiff arms of this woman who could not
show me tenderness. We speak the language
of hunger, which worries me since I can't
understand what her hunger is.
                                        In the Corot, the woman
gathers flowers and herbs, which I glean to decode
their soothing scents. *I've heard,* I tell my soldiers,
the way to one's heart is through sustenance. But
I like the word *manna*, the soft maternal sound of it.

My grandmother, when we are alone,
is not the woman others see.

And so, I continue to gather arsenal, peering
through the bars at the ironed hem of her
floral dress, watching the steam of white doves
escape her heavy-lidded pot.

Dream Where I Find My Roof

I dream it, the dream my yearning self
        sleeps for. I'm at my own

birthday party celebrating with
        all the father figures I have known—

the nurturers who've made me feel loved,
        and my true father, Uppo, who haunted me

with his absence. They file in hand in hand—
        black tuxedos, white shirts, bowties,

a few, those who taught me to be reckless,
        buttons undone, ties loosened—

ready to take the floor for the *dabke*,
        line dance born of Lebanese villagers

gathered on housetops with drums
        and ouds—music to stomp straw,

mud, and twigs into sturdy roofs—
        protection from the volatile sky.

As other guests arrive, I turn
        to greet them—just long enough

that when I look back, the men are gone!—
        before I could tell them how their

presence blessed me with sheltering
        hours. But how I was left with Sittu, always Sittu

who viewed this granddaughter with eyes
        sharp as bee stings, her words termites

gnawing at my roof. How even then, I clung
        to her apron to learn the language of food

having been taught the language of hunger.
        I would tell you how it felt to only *imagine* you,

as the night sky opened its inviting buffet of stars
        that never drew close enough to feed me.

Another Dream About Not Having Children

A scarab crawls down the wall and it's
luminescent—the color of the moon
when you can almost touch it. I take
a closer look. Usually I'm wary around
leggy insects but this one wears tiny
red sneakers. When it reaches the floor

I notice its small top hat along with
the little candy cane it lifts up and down
rhythmically. It all seems possible
as Fred Astaire dancing on the ceiling
to "You're All the World to Me." I follow
this little creature—Alice chasing

the rabbit, on one hand wishing
to catch it yet not wanting to interrupt
the performance that has now woken
the attention of a deceased lover, one
I couldn't commit to and still miss.
He too is animated, and like the beetle

has no regard for time. Then, because
I hesitate—torn between the sight
of a ghost who lives forever inside me
and the charm of this insect with
an impossibly short life—in what seems
like an instant, they both get away.

La Familia

after a collage by Lisa Ortega

Papa holds a piece of sky, Andromeda,
daughter of Cepheus who learned the only way
to save his kingdom was to sacrifice *his* daughter
who was then stripped and chained
to a rock by the sea.
                           See how the mother carries
the sea in her belly? Her orchid breasts, symbol
of strength. She brings the fragrance of vanilla,
an offering of love and *grātiās.*
                           This family floats
on rice-paper terrain, its vastness flecked with risk,
with hope, ready to be collaged into the fabric
of América, *el asilo,* refuge, sanctuary—
unhinged from chains of poverty, the way
Perseus, slayer of monsters, set Andromeda free.

Here, the young daughter is the future, dressed in
a mosaic of crimson—color of Mars, shade
of the unknown. The family's featureless faces,
a tabula rasa, ready to be written with
Veri qui a dignum, any truth that is worthy.

The Cinematic Nature of Nightmares

"Say you hoped to tame something wild and stayed calm and inched up . . ."
—Kay Ryan, "On the Nature of Understanding"

A man marches across my lawn, toward my door, wielding a gun. Doesn't say

boo. Loose curls, collared shirt tucked in, he says, "You

are about to freeze in the presence of danger." Of course, I hoped

in my head—in my actual frontal lobe—I might persuade him to

reframe that to, *12,000 years ago Lake Michigan was covered in ice*, a tame,

more in-the-grand-scheme-of things scenario. Then I'd say something

to appeal to his bruised childhood: "I didn't read *Where the Wild*

Things Are until I was much older—I'm one of those late bloomers—and,

OK, I still hope to flower fully." He considers this, likely because I stayed

wider-scope. Cut to voice-over: *Out of nowhere she found this calm*

and yielded to his latent needs asking if he'd like his forehead rubbed. And

he figures, *Damn, I can't get that if I shoot her.* Miraculous—the way I inched

into his waning heart. Oh, and he tells me I'm beautiful—right before I wake up.

Swamped

Trying to remember an event, my mother pauses, says
I'm having trouble with the figuring out part of my brain.
Her mind once a river, now a swamp: slow moving,
sometimes stagnant.
                          A river's trickle evokes home
movies we never had, the silent 8mms with the *click, click, click*
of time passing—a kid's birthday party, or families opening
Christmas packages. Never moments like the day

I got caught smoking at twelve. Can't remember
if the cigarettes were Parliaments or Tareytons,
the names all sounded important even regal.
Ads featuring well-dressed folks lighting up,
taking a drag blowing their cares away.

Fearing the consequences of being outed I ran away
before my mother got home from work, slept
on the plant-studded bank of the Rouge River.
The ground was hard, noises unfamiliar, and
the night grew cold. When I exhaled, the air
turned to fog that resembled the smoke
that brought me there, as if there were no place
for guilt to hide.
                          I missed the softness
of my bed, that is, the feeling of home. Last
night I dreamed mom was the fog gathered
on the window. When I got too close, the warmth
of my breath made her disappear.

If grief inhabits a swamp, then memory is a river
that floods it, the brimming waters saturating,
littering the land with alluvial debris,
leaving no place to rest, no terra firma.

I want to remember the things you said
when I was younger, remember how we were
in a room together just talking. But I've always
had a poor memory and today you sound
like a child, sweet, innocent.
                              I guess I could
make it all up, lie to myself just to feel better.
But right now the figuring out part of my brain
isn't working that well because everywhere I look,
everything I see is a swamp.

How to Make Horror Films

"The only way to get rid of my fears is to make films about them."
—Alfred Hitchcock

Alfred, a Humpty-Dumpty of a man, lay
in a hospital bed remembering how his mother
forced him to stand at the foot of her bed
for hours, à la Norman Bates in *Psycho*.

And though he was afraid of clowns, his parents
hired one to entertain him. The unkempt buffoon
looked like he'd been on a bender as he performed
a trick with a single egg, fumbling the fleshy orb
around his stubby fingers to make it disappear—
it never did.
            Once, Alfred's father sent his
five-year-old son to the police station with a note
requesting he be locked up for ten minutes for bad
behavior. The chief put him in the cell saying,
"That's what we do to naughty boys,"
which explains Alfred's abiding fear of police
so much so he wouldn't even learn to drive.

Another fear—eggs. "The white round thing
without any holes." An egg yolk breaking
and spilling its yellow liquid. "Blood," he said,
"was positively jolly by comparison."

Even after more than fifty films,
most of which he was afraid to watch,
all the king's horses all the king's men could
never put Hitchcock together again.

Dementia Walks into a Bar

De men are in dementia, don't cha see,
and should you anagram it further you'll find
a *dime* for a *matinee* with a *maiden*
who isn't a *meanie*. All sound better
than Alzheimer's. Al's Heimer. What's
a heimer, anyway? Urban dictionary says,
a girl who plays a guy without having
any real interest in him. Poor Al. What about

jingleheimer, those annoying tunes you can't
get out of your head? Or, dingleheimer,
a dingbat with a crusty dingleberry mustache,
like Hitler's. And there's dingledodie Kerouac's
word to describe those with a madness born
of passion: *But then they danced down the street*
like dingledodies . . .
                                    better than dinglefoot,
that's when you step in dog shit with bare
feet and get a case of the dinglefoot,
which is what I'm doing now, stepping in it.
Because dementia is no laughing matter,
even though I'm trying to find ways for it to be.

Have you heard the one about the guy who sees
a doctor for a checkup? "I have bad news:
you have cancer and dementia." The man replies,
"Well, at least I don't have cancer."

Art Critic Robert Hughes Finally Writes About Goya

> "Fantasy abandoned by reason produces impossible monsters; united with
> it, she is the mother of the arts and the origin of marvels."
>
> —Francisco Goya, *Los Caprichos*

For years he tried to write about Goya,
something was missing, hard to define,
a horror he couldn't connect with,
until he lay helpless, crushed in a wreck.

Something was missing, hard to define
call it *fantasy abandoned by reason*—
crushed, near death in the wreckage,
he encounters impossible monsters.

Fantasy abandons reason
amid war's pain and suffering,
Goya's impossible monsters,
contorted, grotesque and pleading.

Amid Hughes's pain and suffering,
his demons have finally found him
contorted, grotesque and pleading,
bones broken all over his body.

His demons pay him a visit—
Madrid gangs mock and taunt him,
bones crushed all over his body
he sees *Satan Devouring His Son*.

Madrid gangs mock, taunt him,
tortured souls of pain and disaster
who saw Satan devouring their sons.
What a wimp I was, what a fool!

His soul spared of pain, disaster—
for years he couldn't write about Goya.
What a wimp I was, what a fool, he said
of the horror he couldn't connect with.

The Man Who Lost His Words

A man who uses words and uses them well
to speak, to write, to counsel others, has no words
to express what can't be seen. Despair his one
companion as he drives miles to the woods,
leaving his car along the forest's edge. He leaves
his wallet, his leather jacket, and his pain inside
the car by the woods where it is night and stars are words
he can't define. And though the oaks, the pines are green
when moonlight penetrates the woods, it means nothing
to the man who no longer thinks about the word that once
meant green. He's driven north, his heart on empty,
mind too full to hear the names of work and home
or what to eat or what to wear or what to be. It doesn't
matter that he is missed by the wife who knows his words,
words of anger, words of sadness, words of love. Or
by the clients who seek his counsel, words of comfort
words of praise, words that once filled his clinic rooms
North in remote woods his mind becomes a thing remote,
darkness the only word left to guide him. And like the ink
that forms the lines that form the words he knew as bonds,
he follows darkness into the woods until every single word
spells silence. He sits alone beneath a tree, blending in
with the dark, a blotter soaking ink, night around him
and inside him. He is cold, and it feels right to disappear
into the dark without his wallet, without his phone, without
his words. Lights flicker at his home, helicopters,
and police cars searching for the man whose words
are missing from the kitchen, from the bedroom
from the office. This man absorbed by night,
the ink of darkness spilling over into the rooms where
loved ones wait with worry and with sorrow. On this night
he does not see the way his wife weeps with his children—
and when the searchlights shine on trees, he does not see
the trees are green or that the red lights from the ambulance
swim like fish lost in the sky. On the ride to the ER where
blankets warm his frigid limbs, he doesn't care that people
wait to hear the words that bring him back. Words lost deep
in the woods where it is dark as he is numb, they cannot see
he understands they cannot see.

In the Company of Sufferers

My analyst says I'm addicted to suffering,
says we learn our worth and I learned
I deserve to suffer. I was schooled by mother

whose body has been a reliquary for pain.
And grandma who fed on the fruit of betrayal,
her words often flavored with its bitterness.

It's not that I want the suffering. I've been in therapy,
after all. Then again, therapy makes you suffer,
forces you to rehash the yeast of suffering.

No consolation, others who've been analyzed
longer than I still suffer, trying to assign reason
to it, measuring fairness and purpose in the dark.

Victor Frankl, existentialist sufferer, says
we discover meaning by doing a deed,
finding value, and by suffering. Woody Allen,

Sisyphus of sufferers, says, *to love is to suffer.*
To avoid suffering, one must not love.
But then one suffers from not loving.

Therefore, to love is to suffer; not to love
is to suffer. I say suffering is a boulder
you carry on your back. At night you plop it

onto your chest, haul it around in your dreams,
and wake exhausted. My analyst says I can't take
a compliment. That I put up a wall. Tells me

suffering becomes an expectation we trust
since we gravitate toward the familiar. Asks
what's with the all-black wardrobe?

Some wear suffering as a badge,
fantasize connections to the greats:
Van Gogh, Poe, Kafka, Miró.

But I've made progress—avoiding
tearful TV ads to save sad-eyed puppies,
mewing litters of kittens. I'm sure

the therapist is right when she says
I'm on empathy overload. Why else
would I tolerate emotional vampires—

psychopaths, soul-gobbling
narcissists, making excuses for why
they don't play well with others.

Perhaps Proust, prolific sufferer
who spent anguished days and
sleepless nights working in a dark studio

had it figured out when he said,
We are healed by a suffering
only by experiencing it in full.

All Day I've Been Trying to Convince Myself

that sweets are the apocalypse of the body proper,
the Sodom and Gomorrah of nutritional decency.
I say, *Hey there Sweetie, hey there Sugar Pie.*
Hey there lady with the size-up pants and
belly of a piñata.
              Would you rather be svelte and fit
or a casualty of the maladies of indulgence? Say no
to cake, buttercream whipped to glory, though
it be moist and welcome as rain during
a dust-bowl drought.
                    Please. Save your bloodstream
from becoming a river that pollutes an entire town—
compromised pancreas, stressed-out adrenals—
for God's sake, woman, save your liver! Yes,

studies show sugar to be addicting as cocaine, so,
consider restraint a test of character. (Though studies
reveal some of us don't test well.) Nevertheless,
time to hike up your big-girl jeans and empty
your pockets: the York Peppermint Patties, buttery
salted caramels, imported Italian Amarelli licorice,
especially violet flavored. I'm not saying

join the gluten-free, Jurassic, juice-cleansing
maniacs. But trust me, you *will* end up like
the preacher tormented by the beautiful nun
with full pouty lips and eyes that could lead you
down the Mariana Trench.
                    He tries to resist
but nothing prevents him from lusting in his heart.
And since that counts too—he gives in, takes
to the bottle, losing her and his purpose
when she's killed in a fire at her new tabernacle.

Think about *that* as you unwrap a Zingerman's
chocolate chip cookie with perfect crispiness-to-chew
ratio. Then feed it to the disposal since
you can't be trusted not to fish it out of the trash.

Ass

Tremulous gibbous moons, sand dunes
of the body's terrain, I'm talking
double bubble entendre—not smart ass,
the know-it-all, the wiseacre—more
cheek to cheek, a tango as it were,
the stuff of rumba, samba, mambo—
parallel yet unparalleled in synonymy.

Call it: buttocks, butt, booty, behind, backside,
bum, buns, bedonkadonk, arse, can, cheeks,
hind-end, haunches, heinie, keister, glutes,
rump, gluteus maximus (or minimus) tail feather,
rear, junk-in-the-trunk, posterior, patootie,
tail, stern, seat, tooshie, tuchus, tush,
apple bottom, backpack, moneymaker,
rear end, duff, fanny, derriere.

Describe it as: voluptuous, large, firm,
fine, jiggly, bouncy, flabby, saggy,
workhorse of the body, a loyal constant,
cushioner of the fall, protector of coccyx,
defender of tailbone.
                    Sitting on it too long,
ill advised. You might wanna move yours,
get your ass in gear, avoid a kick in the ass.

Often maligned, called skinny, scrawny, sorry,
fat, wide, huge, and though tight jeans might beg
the question, *do these make my butt look big?*
Let's be honest, it makes itself look big.

Some identify with it, I'm an ass man,
which is different than saying, I'm an ass,
though often said by one.

There are isometrics to tighten it, surgery
to lift it, fill it—some are labeled with it:
bad ass, tight ass, horse's ass, half-ass, asshole.

Some feel like one, others make an ass
of themselves, do things ass-backwards,
bass-akwards.
                    There are those who have
their head up their ass, some drag theirs,
some would have you kiss their
sweet one goodbye, think they are
kick ass, cool.
                    You don't want yours
too large, but then again, small is also
a problem, no ass, flat, pancake ass.

The point is your ass is on the line,
you have to cover your ass, watch your ass,
be wary of ass kissers and hard asses.

People fall flat on theirs, some freeze theirs off,
work theirs off, get theirs kicked while others
gamble and lose theirs.
                    Ass, a one syllable,
not one-note wonder. Call it the orchestral
symphony of the body, the wind section,
the flute and toot, heralding trumpet—
the tuba, the coda, the end that never ends.

Pulp Sugar *in the Voice of Captain Friday*

1- Cupcake Rialto

It was one of those trendy shops—cupcakes displayed like expensive jewelry. "Real butter?" I asked. Because I couldn't take another waxy Crisco betrayal—the cloying makes you feel cheap. She didn't answer. So, I took a bite, found out she was all satin and buttercream—Italian meringue—rich, unctuous, not too sweet. "You have one hell of a mouth feel," I said, thinking she must be partial to a paddle on her mixer—I ordered two—knowing it would cost me in more ways than one.

2- Torched by an Angel

I spoon-tapped him just once and he cracked like seven years bad luck. Maybe I was superstitious but beneath his burnt sugar exterior, he was smooth, spoke with a French accent, said his name was Brûlée, Crème Brûlée. And he was loaded—with calories but he was refined. Said he'd been to Madagascar for vanilla. His creamy center, silky as yolks—a perfect foil to the smoky crunch of his caramelized shell. I'd heard he could be addictive, but once I got through to that firm custard heart—I was willing to take my chances.

3- Donut Made My Brown Eyes Blue

She wore a cloak of rich ganache over her bronzed dough. Underneath, it was hard to tell what she was about. I coaxed her open and she spilled, said she was Caramel Chocolate. I knew she was fresh, the way the cake seemed warm even after it was cool. Noticed how the caramel, smooth and glossy, oozed from her tender heart. She warned me that she was seasonal, only available for a limited time. Said I'd miss her when she's gone. Some called her cheap, only a dollar, but to me she was worth much more.

4- Cheesecake Any Way You Slice It

He stood a good six inches tall not including his pastry crust. I asked him where he was from. He said New York by way of Philly. But he wasn't all cream cheese and eggs. This guy was pampered, took hot water baths for hours. Said it takes time to be this smooth. He had eye appeal alright, but I told him I wasn't superficial. So, I planned on a taste, one bite. Maybe it was the hint of lemon zest, the scent of bourbon vanilla, or that luxurious density lingering on my tongue, but I couldn't forget him, even after he was all gone.

5- Mousse with a Bod for Sin

Decadent, sinful, even her name was exotic—Theobroma Cacao, born in the trees of the Amazon Rainforest. She was intense, 85 percent dark chocolate. And she got around—a mixing bowl, liked to be whipped into airy submission with luxurious cream, egg whites, and more than a pinch of sugar. I knew she had a reputation for showing off. Found her posing in a chilled wine glass with a tall stiletto stem. Maybe it was too soon to admit this pitter-patter was love. But if this is wrong, I don't want to be right.

Opera Buffa

At La Dolce Vita, in the village,
the gnocchi, so light they lift
off the fork, float like a cloud
in your mouth. Marinara so fresh
it ripens the tomatoes right on your tongue.

Clemenza's in the kitchen
stirring the sauce telling everyone
he really doesn't eat that much,
it's the fumes that have permeated
his body, made him fat.

My date Antonio closes his eyes
after each bite, groans, "Marone,
this is as good as my mother's."
He lays his folded napkin
on the empty plate and slumps
in the chair while I, having saved room,
crane my neck looking for the waiter.
"What, you want dessert too?"

He seems surprised. "*I'd like to
see what they have*," though
I've committed it to memory.

"Aren't you satisfied?" he adds.
Am I satisfied? I think to myself.
It's bad enough we have to die,
that I'm not taller, that my metabolism
is molto lento, but to dine with someone
who is indifferent to a chilled plate
of panna cotta, silky, quivering cream
adorned with fresh berries, or torta strega, cake
perfumed with liqueur, filled with pastry cream,
and finished with hazelnut meringue.

I cannot live on lasagna alone and
the fact that Antonio doesn't sense this
threatens our chance for a future.

The waiter smiles as he unravels
the dessert menu, handwritten
on rough brown craft paper.
Tiramisu, Umbrian apple tart
Seville orange sorbetto . . .
"This is so beautiful," I say,
ordering the panna cotta.
"May I keep the menu?"
"Of course, Signora. And you sir?"

"No. Nothing for me, just a cup
of espresso."

Oh Antonio, Antonio what are you
thinking? How can I trust a man
who doesn't like sweets?

At La Dolce Vita what could have
been the start of a beautiful romance—
snapped like a string on a Stradivarius!

Bone Bone Frisson

Infatuation—
it's Life Savers
gone Altoids,
the full throttle
of mint, wild groves
of mentholated spears,
green as the leaves in juleps.

Give me an icy river
in June, a tall drink
of cool mist, the sheer
descent of the falls.

Hey, it's me,
Tarzana in Juneau!
winging like a tundra swan.

I saw you in my Turkish coffee cup,
swilled you into being.

Let's blow this desert, you said,
throw on your city slicker and hop on!
This, this is the polar express.

Ever notice how polar bears look
at one another? Tenderness in bulk.

The word for bear in French is *ours*,
add the *y* and make me yours.
I'll shamelessly rhyme
for you in any language.

These are the risks we must take.

So, button me open
and zip me down—
it's cold out but I'm on fi-ya!

Man and Flambé

An old flame had a taste for showy flambés
       back when blazing desserts were theater for the in-crowd.
He loved the tableside flare of cherries jubilee, sugared orbs

dressed in rum, set aflame—a billowy bobble whipped up
       for Queen Victoria. And baked Alaska, its fluffy meringue
scooped out for ladles of cognac to singe the eggy igloo.

No meal was complete without café diablo, clove-studded orange
       peel swimming in a cauldron of burning brandy.
What is it about men and fire? The Moors fanned culinary flames

centuries ago, spreading them across Europe. Glowing
       plum pudding lit up Christmas tables in England.
Three shots of spirits ignited for *omelette au rhum* in France.

My eternal flame is mesmerized by the sight of bananas foster—
       caramelized Cavendish drenched in rum and liqueur—torched
with a heavy *poof*. Booze gone combustible, not for warmth,

but the right-before-your-eyes spectacle of harnessing
       a sultry inferno. Let's face it, next to lust, if ever a noun runs
rampant, fire wins. Which explains man's need to conquer it, to be

Vulcan riding toward the volcano. My guy finds any excuse
       to nurture embers in the wild. Brandishing a flaming marshmallow-
topped twig like an Olympic torch still sets his world on fire.

The Home Shopping Network Waxes Poetic

Out of the corner of my eye I see a guy
on TV flaunting amenities at his hotel.
He picks up a queen bed pillow, stroking
each side. "We have these lovely *two-sided*
pillows in every room!" I stop what I'm doing,

can't wait to see what other amenities
this hotel has to offer—tables with legs,
doors with knobs? Reminds me
of hawkers on shopping networks,

the host pushing faux-alligator shoes
that "leave realistic animal footprints
in snow or soft ground," praising
colors you won't find anywhere else:
sarcoline, flesh-colored to make your legs
look longer, flirty-orange coquelicot,
and "our most popular choice smaragdine"
in shades of emerald. How can one resist

a bevy of lovely presenters who've never
met a product they couldn't elevate with
a slow reveal, infectious enthusiasm,
and gobbledygook? Imagine what they
could do for other things folks don't realize
they need, like poetry.

"Today's special feature, a lovely sestina
written by the poet laureate of Zug Island.
Each stanza comes with six lines featuring
the same powerful end words in a dazzling
array of combos. And, for the next thirty-six
minutes we'll include the final three lines,
the envoi, also known as tornada! Each stanza

can be purchased separately, but order now
and we'll send not one, not two, but all six plus
the envoi for the low price of your shopping addiction!
As an added bonus, your sestina will be printed
in poetic hues such as glaucous, the powdery blue-gray
coating on plums, or falu, the deep red shade of a barn
at dusk, or my favorite, Xanadu, the gray-green
of a mature philodendron.

Best of all, poems are trending as the new
black & white, or what we like to call
papa midnight. They're small enough to fit
in your pocket, have toe-tapping rhythm,
and only take minutes to read.
                                                                    I know what you're
thinking. What if my attention span needs even shorter
works? Well, stay tuned! The next hour features our
five-line limericks reproduced from genuine 11th-century

manuscripts. These amazing bite-sized poems come
engraved in happy-dance green on authentic Irish mugs.
Best of all, we'll throw in the handle, free of charge."

Pimping the Faltering No

The word, a brief consonant,
whiff of a vowel. It never comes
easy—unless I use it to deny
myself—breathe life
into the death of me.

Even in ready-aim-shoot stance,
the mirror doesn't recognize
my clumsy rehearsals,
N flounders, *O* falls away.

Me: You there! Scissoria.
Look at me!

Some find eye contact
an affront. Some call it a lie.

The mother of an old lover
who often averted her gaze
passed the trait on to her son.
When he said *I love you*,
he spoke to the firmament.

Imagine being the universal you.

Everything, even suffering, takes practice.

Come on. Regardez.

I am your crystal ball.
Ask me anything . . .

Decathect

I wear shades to forget light
but still recall the hanging moon,
how it shone on your face
in whisky dark.

I pinch my nose among the roses
but the thorns still perfume
the air in every room
that held your breath.

I press a cold spoon to my mouth
to freeze the lip of my resolve,
swing a hammer at the panes
to change the view.

I use the crayon you once used
to color doors of my heart shut,
fade the songs of meadowlarks
to barely blue. The way your touch

traveled through me like a blessing
for the damned, I watch the sea
extend to shore its watery hand.

Self-Portait as Autopsy

SUBJECT: Caucasian female seasoned with Mediterranean salt.

AGE: Affinity for the Renaissance, La Belle Époque, and Summer of Love.

HEIGHT: Tall as Cassiopeia.

EYES: Filled with the searching gaze.

HAIR: Shades of flowering tobacco.

DISTINGUISHING FEATURES: Strawberry birthmark, shape of home.

BRAIN: Weight: 3 ounces. Heavier when filled with the ruminations of guilt.
Occipital lobe: Evidence of Picasso's observation: we see one thing at a time, a nose, an eye versus the entire visage. Might explain why the subject favored Mr. Potato Head over Barbie, who couldn't turn her smile into a frown.
Frontal lobe: reveals a conscience of the Catholic ilk though subject is not Catholic.

HEART: Typical 10 ounces. Surface: fossil hard. Core: maudlin. Scars date back to childhood, consistent with wounds that open like the Roman gates of Janus.

SOUL: Poet/physician Duncan MacDougall, who weighed bodies immediately before and after death, says 21 grams. Considering the soul's definition: one's moral compass of identity, subject wavered, especially when no one was looking.

FLESH: Skin, thin as any declaration on parchment.

FINDINGS: a) Multiple contusions of the heart.

b) Brain fatigue from attempting to hold onto reason.

CONCLUSION: In an effort to subvert emotion through logic, subject traversed the brain like an ant colony plowing cracks in the sidewalk. Surface labyrinth, resulting from subject's effort to sow more desirable paths proved no match for primal grooves which remained very much intact. Heart remained warm.

Crush

The first cake I baked was for Bill,
the widower who lived upstairs
in our duplex. I was eleven,
and having been fatherless
since the age of seven, failed
to recognize the distinction
between romantic love and paternal
affection. Babysitting his young children,
I imagined myself with Bill, fantasized
this cake would make him swoon
the way men lusted for Betty Crocker.
I ripped open the box, dropping shiny
eggs, water, and oil into the pale powdery
mix, stirring until the batter was smooth.
The sweet scent enveloped me as I waited
near the warm oven imagining Bill's arms
wrapped around me. When the cake cooled,
I creamed butter for frosting, adding vanilla,
milk, and sugar, unaware you can't substitute
granulated for the powdered variety. Later,
I listened for his footsteps and ran the cake
upstairs, watched him cut a large piece.
Watched as he lifted the fork to his mouth
pretending not to notice the crunch of hard,
sugary bits echoing above his praise.

The Gift

after the movie Puzzle

We realize Agnes is throwing her own party
         when she brings out the cake she's baked
to blow out the candles she lights. We see her serve

guests and finally herself before responding
         with a practiced smile to hoots of
"Honey, bring us another beer."

Later that night she sits alone in the spotless
         dining room, breathing a sigh that could fill
a party balloon. Surveying the packages, she pauses

to study a box that contains a 1000-piece puzzle.
         Agnes pours it onto the table flipping each piece
right-side up, and without organizing them in

any logical manner, assembles the entire puzzle in no time.
         Thinking it may be a fluke, she breaks it apart
and proceeds to solve it again.

We see surprise unfold in her countenance—
         upward turn of mouth, leafy flutter of eyes,
an awakening that comes when you do something

you didn't know you could do. I imagine a jigsaw
         of a map, the roads, spokes leading from
a comfortable suburb to the frenetic hub of the big city

when she secretly hops a train to Manhattan
         in search of more challenging puzzles. She extends
each visit, returning later and later, forgetting

to prepare dinner or buy the cheese her husband likes—
         dumping a new puzzle on the table, making
short work of it. Her surprise soon replaced with pride,

confidence, no forced smiles with identifiable edges,
         but irregular expressions, double-wing shapes
tessellating across a tableau free of defined borders.

Her hand sifts through the pieces, eager to assemble
         a new picture without the regret of having
built an entire puzzle around a missing piece.

Agnostic

In the bath a spider crawls along the ledge.
It's tiny enough that it doesn't scare
this arachnophobe. Isn't that the way
fear works, the smaller the threat the less
a reason to run? Unlike the huge or maybe
average wolf spider that cornered me
in the kitchen. In a panic I reached for
Easy-Off, sprayed the hirsute carapace
into an igloo of chemical foam.
Drenched, seemingly undaunted,
the fizzy white dome skittered across
the linoleum toward me as I fled,
as if from Godzilla.
                              But here in my tub
this little guy freezes. And not knowing
what else to do with my ease, this power,
I count his legs, confirming he is anatomically
correct. Unable to take my eyes off him,
I count again, this time in Spanish. But when
I reach for the washcloth—*poof*, he disappears!
No sign of him on the ledge or tub. I check
for holes in the grout—nothing. In its absence
the creature grows, becomes ubiquitous.
And isn't that how faith works?
A reason to believe—a reason not to.

How Much Freedom Do You Give the Fly
You Caught for a Pet?

Truth is, you cannot keep him
captive forever. For one thing,
like us, he has but a short time to live,
in his case roughly 14 days. His

tropical makeup won't survive
much below 36 degrees. And then
he must contend with thousands,
dare I say millions of other flies;

the feckless flies who've landed
who knows where, the drifters
that dwell among stray dogs,
the bodacious horsefly. So, how far

can he wander to be free to hum
his buzz-saw tune into a napping ear,
or experience the thrill of escaping
the mortal swat of a rolled *NY Times*?

Your hope, he befriends the hovering
fruit fly who may lack the aerodynamism
of a half-pipe snowboarder, or slingshot
projectile, but at least you know

he's near, leaving for a moment
the unattended pasta, to land
on ripe fermenting peaches
and darkly speckled bananas.

Doubling the Entendre

Everything has two meanings
                              and you go for the one   that must be true.
You compare apples to oranges:
                              an exaltation of larks
                              is to the sun slipping off its pedestal
                              as a springboard is to *oops*.
To locate lost mojo—password please.
                    If you say *the mighty river began with a dripping faucet*
you're so close!
                         I like you. I like what you've done <3
How long will you bask in that glow?
                         Because let's be honest   we never are.
You sleep with one eye open   not far from the apple tree
                              measuring the downhill from here
            wondering if Newton ever felt un-Newtonish. (It's not like he *invented*
                                                                              gravity.)
One eye dreams your dreams
                         the other slays them   gladiator style.
Put on your chinked armor and ask yourself
                         how often must you tap your amygdala
to realize it's time
              to stop
                    rounding your shoulders and pontificating (to yourself)?
It's rumination not ruination! Damn it, honey. One nation under . . .
      How is it no one else notices   you are an imposter?

Maybe
      it's cause we needs ya baby
                    we need the stars   and that fleeting twinkle in your eye.

ACKNOWLEDGMENTS

"Agnostic," *Streetlight Magazine*

"All Day I've Been Trying to Convince Myself," *decomP magazinE*

"An Unkindness of Ravens," *The Crucible* (Winner of Crucible Poetry Prize)

"Anatomy Lessons," *Praxis: Gender & Cultural Critiques*

"Anesthesia Awareness," *Soundings East*

"Another Dream About Not Having Children," *Griffin*

"Ass," *Heavy Feather Review*

"Bone Bone Frisson," *Mantis*

"Close," *Mudlark*

"Crush," *The MacGuffin*

"Decathect," *Crack the Spine*

"Dementia Walks into a Bar," *Radar Poetry*

"Doubling the Entendre," *descant*

"Dream Where I Find My Roof," *Cordite Poetry Review*

"Excuses for Not Falling in Love," *Griffin*

"Extirpation," *El Portal*

"Guilt Masquerades as Pleasure at the Venetian Ball of Sweets," *Red Wheelbarrow*

"Heartbreak Number One," *SLAB*

"How Much Freedom Do You Give the Fly You Caught for a Pet?" *Full Circle Journal*

"I Feel Like I Sprained My Damn Heart," *Steam Ticket*

"In the Garden of the Universe," *Forge*, also *cho: contemporary haibun online*

"In the Company of Sufferers," *Glint Literary Journal*

"Instructions for the Aspiring Rock Star, Circa 1894," *Griffin*

"La Familia," *Gingerbread House*

"My Drowned Lover's Soul Inhabits My Dog," *Streetlight Magazine*

"My Mother Cuts Me Open and Finds an Apple Inside," *Existere—Journal of Arts & Literature*

"Neruda in My Kitchen," *The MacGuffin* (Pushcart Nominee)

"Opera Buffa," *Rattle*

"Palm Reading Detroit," *Peninsula Poets*

"Planetary Biology at Beaumont Hospital," *CHEST Journal: American College of Chest Physicians*

"Refugee," *Mizna*

"Pulp Sugar," *The MacGuffin*

"Saudade," *decomP magazinE*

"Self-Portrait as Autopsy," *Prism*

"Sex, Guilt, and Counter Espionage, Sinatra Style," *Griffin*

"Snow Falls Off Bare Branch," *Streetlight Magazine*

"Solving for X," *Beecher's Magazine*, now *LandLocked*

"Swamped," *Radar Poetry*

"Tatterdemalion," *Cumberland River Review*

"The Art of Kintsugi," *Bamboo Ridge Press*

"The Cinematic Nature of Nightmares," *The MacGuffin*

"The Fist on Jefferson Avenue Meets Isaac Newton," *Mudlark*

"The Girl from Ipanema Visits Detroit, 1964," *RESPECT: The Poetry of Detroit Music*

"The Home Shopping Network Waxes Poetic," *The MacGuffin*

"The Man Who Lost His Words," *North Atlantic Review*

"The Philosophical Nature of Peeps," *The Minnesota Review*

"When the Heart Needs a Stunt Double," *Columbia: A Journal of Literature and Art*

"Ya'aburnee," *Mantis*

"You Say the Kitchen Is Your Country," *decomP magazinE*

My deepest gratitude for the support of amazing Editor-in-Chief Annie Martin and to the excellent team at WSU Press including Carrie Downes Teefey, Kristina Stonehill, Emily Nowak, and Jamie Jones. I am so grateful for the unwavering support of longtime peers and dear friends Mary Jo Firth Gillett, Mindy LaPere, Christine Rhein, and Carol Was. And to M. L. Liebler, Shannon Johnson, and my husband Lou DeCillis, I can't thank you enough.